What's in Your Food?™

RECIPE FOR DISASTER

Fast Food

Stephanie Watson

rosen publishing's
rosen
central®

New York

*To my mother, who instilled in me a respect for healthy eating,
and who never once took me to a fast-food restaurant*

Published in 2008 by The Rosen Publishing Group, Inc.
29 East 21st Street, New York, NY 10010

Library of Congress Cataloging-in-Publication Data

Watson, Stephanie.
Fast food / Stephanie Watson.—1st ed.
    p. cm.—(What's in your food? Recipe for disaster)
Includes bibliographical references and index.
ISBN-13: 978-1-4042-1416-3 (hardcover)
1. Convenience foods. 2. Junk food. 3. Nutrition. I. Title.
RA784.W4235 2008
613.2—dc22

                                                                    2007023666

Printed in China

Contents

Introduction

Health experts have been saying for years that fast food is bad for people. In February 2003, a filmmaker named Morgan Spurlock decided to perform an experiment to see if that claim was true. He wanted to find out what would happen to his body if he ate nothing but fast food for thirty days.

Spurlock ate every breakfast, lunch, and dinner at McDonald's. He ate everything on the menu at least once, including hamburgers, french fries, and chicken nuggets. Anytime the person behind the counter asked if he wanted the biggest— "Supersize"—meal, he said yes. Spurlock and his doctors tracked what happened to his body. He made a movie of the whole experience, called *Super Size Me* (2004).

At the end of one month, Spurlock's body had changed significantly. He had gained twenty-five pounds (eleven kilograms). He felt tired all the time, and his cholesterol—

Morgan Spurlock captured his fast-food experiment in a movie called *Super Size Me* . When the film premiered in April 2004, it was a big hit with audiences.

the fatlike substance that clogs arteries and can lead to heart attacks—had skyrocketed. He had more of the fats called triglycerides in his blood, and his liver was damaged. His doctor told him that if he didn't stop his experiment soon, he could die.

Spurlock's movie received much attention from film critics and moviegoers. It also caused quite a bit of debate. Health experts said it proved that fast food is unhealthy. People in the fast-food business said it was just a crazy stunt Spurlock did to get people to see his film.

What happened to Morgan Spurlock's body doesn't prove that fast food is unhealthy. Eating fast food for every meal is pretty extreme—most people don't eat nearly that much. But two things are certain. Americans are eating more fast food than they used to eat. And, according to the Centers for Disease Control and Prevention (CDC), people in the United States are fatter, and unhealthier, than they were a few decades ago.

The Obesity Epidemic

Children eat five times more fast food today than they did in 1970, as reported in a 2004 study published in *Pediatrics*. Every single day, one out of three young people aged four to nineteen eats fast food.

At the same time, Americans are gaining weight. Almost 20 percent of children aged six and up were overweight in 2003–2004, according to the CDC. That's three times more overweight children than in the late 1970s. Health experts call this big rise in the number of overweight children an epidemic.

Being overweight can lead to many health problems, such as type 2 diabetes. People who have type 2 diabetes cannot utilize the hormone insulin, which helps the body's cells convert the sugar from foods into energy. When you are overweight, your body has more trouble using insulin. There is also type 1 diabetes, which is caused by a problem with the immune system that damages the cells that make insulin. However, type 1 diabetes is not related to being overweight.

Before 1994, only about 5 percent of children with diabetes had the type 2 kind. But because there are more overweight kids today, 30 to 50 percent of children with diabetes have the type 2 kind, according to the National Diabetes Education Program.

Why do young people seem to be heavier—and unhealthier—than ever before? One reason is that they're not moving as much as they used to. They get a ride to school instead of walking. They play video games instead of sports. They also don't get as much exercise in school. In 1991, almost half of U.S. students took physical education class in school every day. In 2003, only 28 percent took daily gym classes, according to the CDC.

There's also the lure of television. The CDC says that young people between the ages of eight and eighteen sit in front of the TV for more than three hours each day. That's time they could have spent playing or exercising. Watching television is not only making children gain weight, it's also making them want to eat foods that aren't good for them.

Selling Fast Food to You

If you're like most young people, you watch a whopping forty thousand TV commercials per year, according to *The Handbook of Children and Media*. Most of those ads are for toys, cereals, candy, and fast food.

Fast-food restaurants spend millions of dollars a year on their commercials. In the ads, they try to get your attention with clowns and fun characters from your favorite movies and TV shows. They make the

These finger puppets of characters from Disney's *The Lion King* are an example of how fast-food restaurants try to lure children to meals by giving away toys from popular movies and TV shows.

burgers, fries, shakes, and other foods that they sell look delicious.

Ads aren't the only way fast-food restaurants try to get your attention. Many of them have playgrounds. They have special meals for children, and they put toys in their kids' meals from movies such as *Spider-Man 2* and *Shrek*. They do these things to get you to buy their food.

Getting the Balance Right

It's hard to resist fast-food restaurants. After all, the food tastes good. The meals don't cost much. Your

Many fast-food restaurants are adding healthier items, such as roasted chicken, to their menus.

friends probably go there to eat and ask you to come along.

It's easy to go to fast-food restaurants because they're everywhere. You can find them in school cafeterias, airports, malls, and hospitals— just about anyplace you look. Eating fast food is OK once in a while. If you make healthy choices at fast-food restaurants, like ordering salads with low-fat dressing or deli sandwiches instead of burgers, you can eat there more often without a problem.

Remember that your body needs many different types of foods to stay healthy. You need to eat fruits, vegetables, chicken, fish, lean meats, milk products, and grains. If you eat fast-food burgers, fries, and shakes every day, you won't be getting the proper nutritional balance. You may end up with a lot of extra weight and health problems, just as Morgan Spurlock did.

Chapter One

Fast Food Gets Cooking

Unless you've never left your bedroom, you've likely been to a fast-food restaurant at least once in your life, and probably more times than that. If someone asked you, "What is fast food?", you could name places such as McDonald's, Burger King, Pizza Hut, and Kentucky Fried Chicken. You'd most likely say that fast-food restaurants serve burgers, fried chicken, pizza, french fries, milkshakes, and soda. You'd also say that fast-food restaurants are quick and inexpensive.

You'd be right about all of these things. Fast-food restaurants are known for selling certain types of food, such as burgers and fries. They prepare their food in only a few steps to get it to you more quickly, and the food doesn't cost too much.

When you go to a fast-food restaurant, you order your food at a counter or drive-through window. People in the kitchen assemble and wrap up your sandwich, take

A number of fast-food restaurants can often be found in one region, as this highway sign demonstrates, selling everything from burgers to tacos to fried chicken.

your french fries out of the fryer, and dispense your soda or milkshake from a machine. Within a couple of minutes, the counter person puts the food on your tray (or hands it to you in a bag through your car window). Finally, you either carry your food back to your table or take it home.

The experience you have at every one of a fast-food chain's restaurants is almost identical. No matter where you are in the country, if you walk into a Burger King, you can order a Whopper. That Whopper will look and taste the same as the last Whopper you ordered, even if you were at a different Burger King. That's because each Burger King restaurant has pretty much the same menu, and the employees cook and serve the food in a similar way.

Even though the food at each restaurant is the same no matter where you are, the menus have changed quite a bit over the last few decades. Instead of serving just burgers and fries, fast-food restaurants now offer items such as salads, omelets, chili, and baked potatoes. Many restaurants are now adding fruit and fruit juice to their meals as an alternative to fries and soda. Panera Bread, Au Bon Pain, and other modern quick-service restaurants serve higher-quality foods, such as French onion soup and grilled panini sandwiches. Fast food has come a long way since it got its start back in the early twentieth century.

The History of Fast-Food Restaurants

At the turn of the twentieth century, most Americans ate at home. Eating out was something reserved for special occasions. But by the 1940s, the United States was changing. New roads crisscrossed the country. A large number of people owned cars. Americans had more free time than previously to eat out.

Restaurants called drive-ins took advantage of the new American lifestyle. People could drive up to the restaurant and park, and servers called carhops would take the orders and bring burgers, fries, and shakes right to the customers' cars.

In 1937, two brothers named Richard and Maurice McDonald opened a drive-in restaurant in Pasadena,

Myths & Facts

Myth: Ordering a salad at a fast-food restaurant is healthier than getting a hamburger.

Fact: It might seem as though a salad would be better for you than a burger, but that isn't necessarily true. The Southwest Taco Salad at Wendy's has 710 calories and 41 grams of fat (if you get it with sour cream, tortilla strips, and dressing), according to the nutritional information posted on the company's Web site. That's more calories and fat than the restaurant's Big Bacon Classic burger (590 calories, 30 grams of fat). To slim down your salads, you need to order fat-free or light dressing, get your salad with grilled chicken instead of fried, and avoid the extras (such as bacon bits and croutons).

Myth: A cheeseburger, fries, and a milkshake is a balanced meal because it contains dairy, meat, vegetables, and grains.

Fact: Break down this meal, and you'll see that it's anything but balanced and nutritious. Burgers, fries, and shakes are very high in calories, fat, and sodium (salt) and low in vitamins and minerals.

Myth: You have to stop eating fast food to be healthy.

Fact: Every type of food—including fast food—is OK to eat in moderation (unless you have a food allergy). If you normally eat a healthy, balanced diet, going to a fast-food restaurant once in a while can't hurt. Making healthier choices (such as ordering a side salad with low-fat dressing instead of fries and skipping the soda) can make a fast-food meal more nutritionally sound.

California. It quickly became very popular, but within a few years, the brothers realized that their customers wanted something more than just good burgers. Americans were becoming busier than ever before. They wanted quick service, and they wanted it at low prices.

In 1948, the McDonald brothers made a few changes to their restaurant. They got rid of the drive-in feature and created counter service inside. They cut down the menu and started serving only hamburgers, cheeseburgers, french fries, milkshakes, and soft drinks. The kitchen became an assembly line, similar to those used to build cars. One person cooked the burgers, one wrapped them, another made the milkshakes, and yet another worked at the counter. They called this assembly line process the Speedee Service System. It changed the restaurant business forever. A bigger revolution was still to come, though, when the McDonald brothers met a traveling salesman named Ray Kroc.

The Golden Arches

In 1954, Ray Kroc went to McDonald's to sell milkshake mixers. He loved the way the restaurant served food quickly and efficiently. Kroc liked the McDonald brothers' idea so much that he asked them if he could build more McDonald's restaurants.

In 1961, Kroc bought the company for $2.7 million and started opening McDonald's restaurants all over the country. By 1963, he had opened five hundred. Today, there are more than thirty thousand McDonald's restaurants around the world. Each of these restaurants is called a franchise.

Other businessmen liked Kroc's idea and decided to start their own franchises. Harland "Colonel" Sanders sold food out of his gas station before opening Kentucky Fried Chicken in 1952. Carl Karcher sold hot dogs and ran a barbeque restaurant before starting Carl's Jr. in southern California in 1956. Glen W. Bell Jr. went from owning a few taco stands to launching Taco Bell in 1962. Fast food was quickly becoming very popular with American consumers.

The Fast-Food Boom

The success of fast-food restaurants in the 1950s and 1960s had much to do with the way America was changing. Fewer women were staying at home and caring for their children. Because they were working full-time jobs, they had less time to cook.

In 1961, Ray Kroc bought out the McDonald's brothers and launched the McDonald's Corporation.

Krispy Kreme and other fast-food restaurants appeal to families because of their low prices and quick service.

Even though more Americans were working than ever before, a lot of them still couldn't afford to eat out at a restaurant. Fast food cost so little that it was affordable even to people who had very little money.

Fast food was not only cheap to buy, it was also convenient. Restaurants popped up everywhere. The number of fast-food restaurants in the United States jumped from about 70,000 in 1970 to 186,000 in 2001, revealed Morgan Spurlock in *Don't Eat This Book*. Most fast-food restaurants had drive-through windows so that people who didn't have time to go inside to eat could take the food home.

All of these changes added up to bigger and bigger profits for fast-food companies. In 1970, Americans spent about $6 billion on fast food, as noted in Eric Schlosser's book *Fast Food Nation*. By 2005, according to *QSR Magazine*, Americans were spending more than $136 billion per year on fast food.

Chapter Two

How Fast Food Is Produced

You've probably eaten fast food many times, but do you know where it comes from and how it's made? You may be surprised to learn that the food you eat at many fast-food restaurants isn't cooked there from scratch. A lot of it is mass-produced in big factories.

To keep prices low, fast-food restaurants have contracts with different food manufacturers. One company may make all of the french fries for a fast-food chain. Its factories use machines to peel, slice, and process the potatoes. It then freezes and ships the french fries to the fast-food company's restaurants. Another factory may make the burgers. People form the ground beef into patties by hand or with machines, freeze them, and put them into boxes. Salads and fruit slices are prepackaged and ready to serve. Trucks carry frozen foods from the different factories to the chain's restaurants.

Getting the Food to the Bun

Since Ray Kroc started the first chain of McDonald's restaurants around the country, the fast-food business has been set up using his franchise model. Each fast-food chain is made up of individual restaurants, called franchises. The owner of each restaurant pays a franchise fee and a part of the profits to the main company. These payments give the owner the right to use the chain's brand images, ingredients, and recipes. That's why every Taco Bell you visit has a similar interior design and menu.

The way in which fast foods are cooked hasn't changed much since the McDonald brothers invented

Hamburgers and chicken nuggets at a fast-food restaurant are assembled in the kitchen, then placed in a warmer until customers order them.

the Speedee Service System. The process works like an assembly line, with each person in the kitchen responsible for doing a certain job.

A kitchen in a typical fast-food restaurant may run something like the following: One person cooks burgers and pieces of chicken on a grill or in a broiler. Another person puts the burger or chicken on a bun and adds cheese, lettuce, tomatoes, pickles, and sauce. Then he or she wraps up each sandwich and places it under a heat lamp to stay warm until a customer orders it. A third person puts frozen potato slices into a fryer filled with hot oil to cook them into french fries. (Some restaurants combine all these tasks into a single job.)

At the counter, one or several people take the customers' orders. They pour the sodas and milkshakes, take the salads and dressings out of a refrigerator, and pull the cooked sandwiches out of the warmer. Then they collect the money and put the food onto a tray or into a bag for the customer to take to a table or to take home. What people may not realize when they grab their tray or bag, though, is just what they're really eating.

Are There Bugs in Your Burger?

In 1993, hundreds of people became sick and four died after eating hamburgers at Jack in the Box restaurants. The culprits were tiny bacteria called *E. coli* in the burgers. The incident was one of the worst cases of food poisoning in the United States, and it made a lot of people concerned about the safety of fast food.

In 2006, a few Taco Bell restaurants in Philadelphia were closed after several people became ill from eating iceberg lettuce tainted with *E. coli* bacteria.

E. coli is found in the intestines of cows and other animals, as well as humans. Hundreds of different types, or strains, of *E. coli* exist. Most of them are harmless. But a few strains, such as O157:H7 (the same kind that was in the tainted Jack in the Box burgers), can be very dangerous to humans.

Sometimes, when meat is being processed at a meatpacking plant, *E. coli* from the cow's intestines can mix with the ground beef and contaminate it. That ground beef is then shipped to restaurants. If that meat is cooked until it reaches about 160° Fahrenheit (71° Celsius), the heat will kill the bacteria. But if the meat isn't cooked long enough, the people who eat it can get very sick and even die. That's why it's important to always get your burgers cooked "well done."

E. coli can also contaminate vegetables such as bean sprouts, spinach, and lettuce. In November and December 2006, there was an *E. coli* outbreak in which more than seventy customers at Taco Bell restaurants throughout the Northeast became sick from eating shredded iceberg lettuce. The most likely source of the *E. coli* was traced to produce fields in California. (Initial reports indicated that green onions might have been the culprit, but these reports were incorrect.)

Before you panic about eating fast food, however, know that it's very rare for people to get sick at fast-food restaurants. State departments of health regularly inspect restaurants. They make sure that the workers are handling the food safely, the food is being cooked to the right temperature, and the kitchens are clean. The odds of you getting *E. coli* poisoning at a fast-food restaurant are very low. The odds of you eating a high-fat, unhealthy meal, on the other hand, are pretty high if you're not careful.

Big Portions, Unhealthy Ingredients

When McDonald's first opened, it had one size of french fries. Today, that same size of fries is called small, and it contains 250 calories. Since then, McDonald's has added medium- (380 calories) and large-sized (570 calories) fries. It even used to have an item called Supersize fries, which contained 610 calories and 29 grams of fat.

21

This colossal egg sandwich sold at Burger King is a true "whopper": it packs 730 calories and 45 grams of fat.

Portion sizes are getting bigger, and fast-food restaurants are offering people plenty of reasons to eat more. They now have value menus with many foods that cost less than a dollar. They also have meal deals, which include a sandwich, large fries, and medium soda for one low price. These meals are not only big, they're also loaded with extra sugar, salt, calories, and fat.

Much of that fat comes in the form of partially hydrogenated vegetable oils. These oils are made by adding hydrogen to liquid vegetable oils to make a more solid kind of fat. (If you've ever opened a can of vegetable shortening, you've seen what partially hydrogenated vegetable oil looks like.) The fat in partially hydrogenated vegetable oils is called trans fat.

Partially hydrogenated oils are what make french fries taste crispy and delicious, and give pies their rich crust. They also help foods stay fresh longer and cost less for restaurants to use than healthier oils. Since health experts started saying that eating trans fats can cause heart disease, many fast-food restaurants have been trying to switch from partially hydrogenated vegetable oils to healthier oils.

If the added fats, sugar, and salt weren't enough, fast-food restaurants also add chemicals, flavorings, and dyes to make their food look and taste better and last longer. Read the list of ingredients at most fast-food restaurants, and you'll need a science dictionary to know what you're eating. Chemicals such as sodium benzoate (a preservative), red dye #40, and monosodium glutamate (a flavor enhancer) are all common ingredients on some fast-food menus.

Making Fast Food Healthier

Fast food has never been known for being healthy, although the industry has tried in the past to add more nutritious foods to its menus. In 1991, McDonald's launched a burger called the McLean Deluxe. It was made with seaweed extract, and it had half the fat of a regular McDonald's hamburger. The problem was that very few people bought it, so the company dropped it from its menu just five years later. When Taco Bell

23

introduced its Border Lights menu of low-fat options in the mid-1990s, that menu also flopped. Most people didn't buy these foods because they thought low fat meant low taste. So, fast-food restaurants continued to focus on their more popular—and less healthy—items.

Then, in 2001, a journalist named Eric Schlosser wrote a book called *Fast Food Nation*. The book exposed unclean conditions at meatpacking plants that sell to fast-food restaurants. It also described the unhealthy ingredients that go into fast food.

All of this publicity wasn't good for fast-food restaurants. It drew attention to the unhealthy foods they serve. To create a better image for themselves, fast-food chains started to make some changes to their menus.

Wendy's began letting customers choose between french fries and healthier side items such as salad, chili, or a baked potato. Subway offered a kid's meal with a small sandwich, low-fat milk, and apple slices. Other fast-food chains

Two fresh new ways to enjoy your favorite fruits.

New!
Fresh Fruit Bowl & Cup

Excellent source of Vitamin A & C

Many fast-food restaurants have introduced healthier items, such as fruit salads, to their menus.

followed their lead. Most fast-food restaurants now post nutrition information on their Web sites and in their stores to help customers understand what they're eating.

These changes are an improvement, but many of the supposedly healthy foods at fast-food restaurants may not be as nutritious as they seem. For example, one fast-food chain offers a line of sandwiches that contain six or fewer grams of fat. Although these low-fat sandwiches are healthy, not everything on the menu is as nutritious. Many of the restaurant chain's other sandwiches are higher in calories and fat than fast-food burgers.

Even salads aren't always good for you. A chicken salad with bacon, honey-mustard dressing, and croutons contains almost seven hundred calories and nearly fifty grams of fat. That salad has more calories and fat than a bacon cheeseburger. The gourmet-sounding foods at more upscale restaurants aren't always low in fat either. A chicken panini can have more fat and calories than a quarter-pound hamburger.

Chapter Three

Your Body on Fast Food

When you eat fast food, you probably think that it tastes pretty good. What you may not think about are the effects it's having on your body.

What's in Your Fast Food?

Most fast food is loaded with fat, calories, sugar, and salt. Although you need all of these things in small amounts, in large quantities they can do some pretty serious damage to your body. Below are a few of the unhealthy substances you'll find in an average fast-food meal:

- **Fat.** Your body needs some fats for energy and to help it grow. There are good fats and bad fats, though. Unsaturated fats (monounsaturated and polyunsaturated fats), found in fish, nuts, and olives, are good for

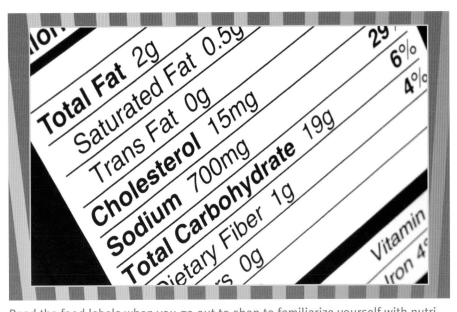

Read the food labels when you go out to shop to familiarize yourself with nutritional content. When you go out to eat, look for foods that are low in saturated fat, trans fat, cholesterol, and sodium.

you. They help lower your cholesterol. Saturated fats and trans fats, found in meat, butter, shortening, and some cooking oils, are bad for you. They raise your cholesterol. Too much cholesterol can clog your arteries—the vessels that carry blood from your heart to the rest of your body. Having clogged arteries is like having clogged drains in your body. They block blood flow throughout your body. If your blood can't get through the arteries the way it's supposed to, your heart has to work harder. When your heart has to work harder, it can become damaged.

- **Calories.** Your body needs energy to function, just like a car needs gas to run. Calories are a measurement of how much energy your body gets from food. If you put more calories into your body than you burn off, your body will store the extra calories as fat. Because fast foods are high in calories, you'd need to do more exercise to burn them off than you would if you ate low-fat foods. (To burn off a 660-calorie fried chicken club sandwich, you'd need to jog for an entire hour.) A 2004 study about the effects of fast-food consumption on children's diets published in the journal *Pediatrics* found that children who ate fast food consumed an extra 187 calories per day than those who didn't eat fast food. For the average child, that would add up to about 6 pounds (3 kg) of added weight per year, according to the study.
- **Sugar.** A large cola at a fast-food restaurant contains 86 grams of sugar and nearly 300 calories. That's about 18 teaspoons of sugar in one cup of soda. When you eat a lot of sugar, it lingers in your mouth. Bacteria feed on that sugar and produce acids, which decay your teeth. In your body, all of the sugar you can't use is converted into fat. That extra fat puts you at risk for obesity, heart disease, and diabetes.
- **Salt.** Sodium (salt) performs some very important jobs in the body. It maintains fluid balance, and it keeps nerves and muscles

working properly. You don't need much to keep all of these functions running smoothly, though. The U.S. Department of Agriculture's Dietary Guidelines for Americans (2005) recommend that people eat no more than 2,300 milligrams (about 1 teaspoon) of salt per day. An order of boneless barbeque wings or a burrito at two popular fast-food restaurants contains more than 2,100 milligrams of sodium each. Having too much sodium in your diet can lead to high blood pressure, which can damage your heart and kidneys.

What Too Much Fast Food Can Do to Your Body

Scientific evidence is showing that fast food, which tends to have a lot of fat and calories, can lead to some pretty serious weight gain. A 2005 study of young adults led by Dr. Mark Pereira, an associate professor at the University of Minnesota, reported that people who ate fast food more than twice each week gained 10 pounds (4.5 kg) more over fifteen years than those who ate fast food less than once every week. You may not think that gaining a few extra pounds can hurt you, but being overweight makes you much more likely to get one of these serious diseases or conditions:

- **Type 2 diabetes.** This disease occurs when the cells of the body can't use insulin properly. If not treated, diabetes can lead to heart disease, blindness, stroke (a blockage in blood flow to the brain), or amputation (surgical removal of a body part, such as a foot). According to Dr. Pereira's study, young adults who often ate fast food didn't respond as well to insulin—the first step toward getting type 2 diabetes.

- **Cancer.** Studies have shown that high-fat diets and obesity can increase your risk of getting several cancers, such as breast, colon, esophageal, and kidney cancer.
- **High cholesterol.** Too much fatty cholesterol in the blood can lead to heart disease and strokes.
- **High blood pressure.** Blood pressure is the force of the blood pushing against the artery walls as it circulates around the body. Being overweight and eating too much salt can raise blood pressure. High blood pressure can lead to a heart attack, heart failure, stroke, and kidney failure.
- **Asthma.** Studies find that overweight people are more likely to get asthma than people of average weight. Asthma causes the airways to become narrowed or blocked, making it difficult to breathe.
- **Mental health problems.** There is evidence that eating fast food can have a negative effect on your brain. A 2005 study led by Rickard L. Sjöberg in Sweden found a significant link between obesity and depression in young

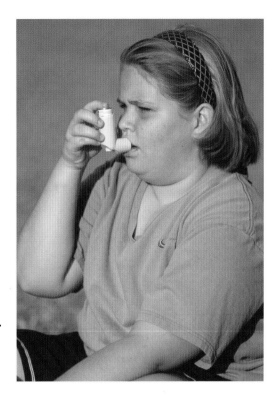

Studies have found that people who are overweight are more likely to have asthma. Many people with this condition need to use an asthma inhaler to help them breathe.

people. Other research has found that attention-deficit/hyperactivity disorder (ADHD) is more common in obese children.

What You're Missing with Fast Food

When you eat a lot of fast food, you not only get more fat, calories, and other unhealthy ingredients, you also miss out on many healthy vitamins and minerals that your body really needs. Children who eat fast food get fewer fruits, green vegetables, and milk. They also consume more meat, french fries, and soda than those who don't eat fast food, according to a 2003 study by Dr. Sahasporn Paeratakul.

Compare foods and you can easily see which ones pack a bigger nutritional punch. A small order of french fries has none of the vitamin A and only 6 percent of

Sodas are a staple at fast-food restaurants, but if you drink them instead of milk, you'll be missing out on bone-building calcium and vitamin D.

the vitamin C you need in one day, plus thirteen grams of fat. A half-cup (seventy-eight grams) of cooked broccoli, on the other hand, has no fat and contains 30 percent of the vitamin A and 80 percent of the vitamin C you need each day.

An eight-ounce (one cup) glass of skim milk has 30 percent of the calcium you need in a day and 25 percent of the vitamin D. The same size cup of soda has no nutrition. It's just sugar, water, and flavoring. Considering that most of your bone mass (especially in girls) is built before you reach the age of eighteen, drinking soda instead of milk can rob your bones of the calcium they need to stay strong. That deficit could lead to fractured or broken bones in the future.

Chapter Four

Fitting Fast Food into a Healthy Lifestyle

Staying healthy doesn't mean that you have to deprive yourself of junk food. You don't have to feel guilty about grabbing a burger and fries, or indulging in a hot fudge sundae on the weekend if you've eaten nutritious foods during most of the week.

According to the 2005 Dietary Guidelines for Americans, published jointly by the Department of Health and Human Services and the U.S. Department of Agriculture, your daily diet should include the following:

- **Vegetables:** Two and a half cups per day, mixing dark green (broccoli, spinach), orange (sweet potatoes, carrots), starchy (corn), and legumes (peas, beans).
- **Fruits:** One and a half cups per day, including a variety such as oranges, apples, grapes, pears, and fruit

juice (make sure the juice is made from 100 percent fruit).

- **Grains:** Six ounces (six slices of bread) per day, with at least half coming from whole grains (whole-wheat bread).
- **Dairy:** Three cups (twenty-four ounces) per day of fat-free or low-fat milk or yogurt, or three ounces of low-fat cheese.
- **Meat/Beans:** Five ounces per day of lean meat (chicken, turkey, fish) and legumes or nuts for protein.

Depending on your gender (boys tend to need more calories, especially as they get closer to puberty) and age, you'll need to eat between about 1,600 and 2,500 calories per day. Only about 25 to 35 percent of the total calories you eat should come from fat. So if you eat about 1,800 calories per day, no more than 630 of those calories should be from fat. The fats you do eat should be the "good" kinds—unsaturated fats from fish, vegetable oils, and nuts.

The Nutrients You Need

In addition to tasting good and relieving your hunger, some types of foods can do amazing things for your body. They can make you stronger, keep your heart pumping like it should, and even fight off disease. Here are some of the nutritional powerhouses that should be a part of your diet:

Nutrient	Benefit	Sources
Calcium	Strengthens bones and teeth	Low-fat milk, yogurt, collard greens, calcium-fortified orange juice
Magnesium	Important for muscle and nerve function, immune system health, and bone strength	Whole-grain breads, almonds, legumes, spinach, soybeans, pumpkin seeds
Potassium	Needed for muscle building, fluid balance, and protein production	Salmon, white beans, spinach, sweet potatoes, tomatoes, broccoli
Vitamin A	Keeps teeth, eyes, and skin healthy	Carrots, cantaloupe, sweet potatoes, liver, milk
Vitamin B_1 (Thiamine)	Helps break down carbohydrates into sugar for energy	Whole-grain cereals, breads and pastas, red meat, fish
Vitamin B_2 (Riboflavin)	Helps break down carbohydrates into sugar for energy and is needed for red blood cell production	Whole-grain cereals and breads, milk, meat, eggs, cheese, legumes
Vitamin B_6 (Pyridoxamine)	Helps break down carbohydrates, fats, and proteins and is used for red blood cell production	Fish, chicken, avocados, liver, garbanzo beans, eggs, red meat, bananas
Vitamin B_9 (Folic acid)	Helps produce the genetic material DNA and hemoglobin (which transports oxygen in red blood cells)	Fortified breads and cereals, leafy green vegetables, liver, fruits
Vitamin B_{12} (Cyanocobalamin)	Makes blood cells and helps nerves function properly	Meat, nuts, legumes, milk
Vitamin C	Important for tissue growth, wound healing, and bone and cartilage repair	Oranges, lemons, berries, green peppers, tomatoes, potatoes
Vitamin E	Protects the body from disease	Vegetable oil, nuts, green leafy vegetables

A healthy diet includes a mix of fruits, vegetables, whole grains, dairy, nuts, and meat or beans.

Making the Right Choices

Eating is all about choice. Until fast-food restaurants completely replace their unhealthy menu items with healthy ones (which may never happen), it's up to you to make good choices about what you're eating. The first choice you have is how often to eat fast food, and moderation is always best. If you're a junk-food addict and you've been going out for fast food three times each week, try weaning yourself off of it. Scale back to once a week, and then to once every two weeks. Use fast food as a treat to reward yourself when you've eaten especially well for a couple of weeks in a row.

10 Great Questions to Ask

1. How often can I eat fast food?

2. What are the healthiest items at fast-food restaurants?

3. What are the least healthy items at fast-food restaurants?

4. How can I modify my fast-food meals to make them healthier?

5. What portion size should I order?

6. How can I use the restaurants' nutritional information as a guide to choose the right foods?

7. Are there any preservatives or other chemicals used in fast foods that I need to be worried about eating?

8. What effects might eating too much fast food have on my body?

9. How can I control my sugar and salt intake when eating at fast-food restaurants?

10. What is the best way to lose the extra weight I've gained from eating too much fast food?

If you eat fast food often, try to cut back to vary your diet. Eating fast food in moderation shows good sense. Instead, you can cook or barbecue at home with family or friends. Choose grilled, broiled, or baked foods rather than fried foods to reduce calories and fat.

You may even try splitting a meal with a friend. You'll save not only calories but money, too.

When you do eat fast food, read the nutritional information (you can also check out the fast-food company's Web site for nutrition information). Focus on foods that are low in calories, fat (especially saturated and trans fats), cholesterol, sugar, and salt. As a general rule, aim for foods that contain 5 percent or less of the daily value of these substances, and stay away from any foods that contain 20 percent or more of the daily value. (Daily value is the total amount of calories you need in one day, and it is listed on the food label. Percent daily value is the percentage of a nutrient the food contains, compared to its total recommended daily value.)

Here are a few tips to guide you when you eat at fast-food restaurants:

- Pick grilled or broiled foods instead of fried.
- Order the smallest portions (get a regular hamburger instead of a quarter-pound burger and you'll save 160 calories).
- Ask for low-fat salad dressing and toppings (such as bacon bits and croutons) on the side, and use them sparingly.
- Whenever possible, substitute a salad or baked potato for french fries.
- Top your sandwich with barbeque sauce, ketchup, or salsa instead of mayonnaise.
- Drink water, milk, or fruit juice instead of soda.

Finally, peer pressure can be a powerful influence, whether it's about drinking, taking drugs, or eating fast food. Don't let your friends sway your decision to eat healthfully. If they want to eat at fast-food restaurants all the time, tell them you're happy to watch them gain weight from the sidelines. You'd rather look good and feel positive about your body.

Glossary

arteries Vessels that carry blood from the heart to the rest of the body.

calorie A unit of energy that is released when the body breaks down food.

carbohydrates Sugars and starches that the body uses for energy.

cholesterol A fatty substance found in certain foods that is carried through the blood. It can build up in the arteries, increasing the risk for heart disease.

daily value The total amount of calories you need in one day as listed on a food label.

diabetes A disease that occurs when the body either does not produce enough of the hormone insulin or does not use it properly.

E. coli   A type of bacteria found in the intestines of humans and some animals. Certain strains of *E. coli* can make people sick.

franchise A business that has an agreement with a big corporation to sell its products and services in a particular area.

hemoglobin The part of red blood cells that carries oxygen to the body's tissues.

high blood pressure A condition that occurs when there is too much pressure from the blood pushing against the walls of the arteries.

obesity A condition in which a person weighs at least 20 percent more than the recommended weight for his or her height and has a body mass index (weight in pounds divided by height in square inches and multiplied by 703) of 30 or more.

overweight Having a body mass index higher than 25 but lower than 30.

partially hydrogenated vegetable oil A solid type of fat used for cooking that is created by adding hydrogen to liquid vegetable oil.

percent daily value The percentage of a nutrient the food contains, compared to its total recommended daily value, based on a 2,000- or 2,500-calorie-per-day diet.

saturated fat A type of fat found in animal products, such as meat, cream, and eggs. Eating large quantities of this type of fat has been linked to heart disease, according to medical researchers.

sodium Another word for salt. The body uses sodium to keep fluids in balance.

trans fat An unhealthy type of fat found in cookies, pies, and french fries. Eating large amounts of trans fats may increase the risk for heart disease.

triglycerides A form of fat that circulates in the bloodstream.

unsaturated fat A healthy type of fat found in fish, nuts, and olives.

For More Information

Action for Healthy Kids
4711 West Golf Road, Suite 625
Skokie, IL 60076
(800) 416-5136
Web site: http://www.actionforhealthykids.org
This is a group devoted to helping kids eat better and
    become more active.

American Dietetic Association (ADA)
120 South Riverside Plaza, Suite 2000
Chicago, IL 60606-6995
(800) 877-1600
Web site: http://www.eatright.org
The ADA helps people eat healthier and prevent
    obesity.

Canadian Council of Food and Nutrition
2810 Matheson Boulevard East, 1st Floor
Mississauga, ON L4W 4X7
Canada
(905) 625-5746
Web site: http://www.ccfn.ca
This Canadian organization is made up of health pro-
    fessionals who help teach the public about food and
    nutrition issues.

MyPyramid.gov
USDA Center for Nutrition Policy and Promotion
3101 Park Center Drive, Room 1034
Alexandria, VA 22302-1594
(888) 779-7264
Web site: http://www.mypyramid.gov
The U.S. Department of Agriculture's MyPyramid.gov
site offers a personal eating plan with recommenda-
tions for the healthy kinds of food and amounts that
are best for your body type and lifestyle. The site
includes a tracker to help you assess your activity
and eating levels.

Slow Food USA
20 Jay Street, No. 313
Brooklyn, NY 11201
(718) 260-8000
Web site: http://www.slowfoodusa.org
Slow Food USA is trying to help people move away
from eating fast foods to eating more old-fashioned,
slow-cooked, natural foods.

Web Sites

Due to the changing nature of Internet links, Rosen
Publishing has developed an online list of Web sites
related to the subject of this book. This site is updated
regularly. Please use this link to access the list:

http://www.rosenlinks.com/wyf/fafo

For Further Reading

Aeseng, Nathan. *Business Builders in Fast Food.*
    Minneapolis, MN: Oliver Press, Inc., 2001.

Cobb, Vicki. *Junk Food* (Where's the Science Here?).
    Minneapolis, MN: Millbrook Press, 2006.

Collins, Tracy Brown. *Fast Food* (At Issue). Farmington
    Hills, MI: Greenhaven Press, 2004.

Harmon, Daniel E. *Obesity* (Coping in a Changing
    World). New York, NY: Rosen Publishing, 2007.

Jukes, Mavis, and Lilian Wai-Yin Cheung. *Be Healthy!
    It's a Girl Thing: Food, Fitness, and Feeling Great.*
    New York, NY: Crown Publishers, 2003.

Nardo, Don. *Understanding Issues—Eating Disorders.*
    Farmington Hills, MI: KidHaven Press, 2003.

Salmon, Margaret B. *Food Facts for Teenagers: A Guide
    to Good Nutrition for Teens and Preteens.* 2nd ed.
    Springfield, IL: Charles C. Thomas, 2002.

Schlosser, Eric, and Charles Wilson. *Chew on This:
    Everything You Don't Want to Know About Fast
    Food.* New York, NY: Houghton Mifflin, 2006.

Silverstein, Alvin, et al. *Diabetes* (My Health). London,
    England: Franklin Watts, 2002.

Watson, Stephanie. *Binge Eating* (Danger Zone: Dieting
    and Eating Disorders). New York, NY: Rosen
    Publishing, 2007.

Bibliography

American Psychological Association. "Television
   Advertising Leads to Unhealthy Habits in Children;
   Says APA Task Force." February 23, 2004. Retrieved
   March 27, 2007 (http://www.apa.org/releases/
   childrenads.html).

Astrup, Arne. "Super-Sized and Diabetic by Frequent
   Fast-Food Consumption?" *The Lancet*, Vol. 365,
   No. 9453, January 1, 2005, pp. 4–5.

Bowman, Shanthy A., Steven L. Gortmaker, Cara B.
   Ebbeling, Mark A. Pereira, and David S. Ludwig.
   "Effects of Fast-Food Consumption on Energy Intake
   and Diet Quality Among Children in a National
   Household Survey." *Pediatrics*, Vol. 113, No. 1,
   January 2004, pp. 112–118.

Centers for Disease Control and Prevention. "Overweight
   and Obesity: Childhood Overweight." February 28,
   2007. Retrieved March 26, 2007 (http://www.cdc.gov/
   nccdphp/dnpa/obesity/childhood/index.htm).

Goodman, Peter S. "Fast Food Takes a Bite out of
   Chinese Culture." WashingtonPost.com. December 26,
   2004. Retrieved April 11, 2007 (http://www.
   washingtonpost.com/wp-dyn/articles/A25868-
   2004Dec25.html).

Harrison, Kristen, and Amy L. Markse. "Nutritional
   Content of Foods Advertised During the Television

Programs Children Watch Most." *American Journal of Public Health*, Vol. 95, No. 9, September 2005, pp. 1568–1574.

Kentucky Fried Chicken. "KFC Ingredient List." Retrieved April 10, 2007 (http://www.kfc.com/nutrition/pdf/kfc_ingredients.pdf).

McDonald's USA. "McDonald's USA Nutrition Facts for Popular Menu Items." Retrieved March 23, 2007 (http://www.mcdonalds.com/app_controller.nutrition.index1.html).

Paeratakul, Sahasporn, et al. "Fast-Food Consumption Among U.S. Adults and Children: Dietary and Nutrient Intake Profile." *Journal of the American Dietetic Association*, Vol. 103, No. 10, October 2003, pp. 1332–1338.

Schlosser, Eric. *Fast Food Nation*. Boston, MA: Houghton Mifflin Company, 2001.

Sjöberg, Rickard L., Kent W. Nilsson, and Jerzy Leppert. "Obesity, Shame, and Depression in School-Aged Children: A Population-Based Study." *Pediatrics*, Vol. 116, No. 3, September 2005, pp. e389–e392.

Spurlock, Morgan. *Don't Eat This Book: Fast Food and the Supersizing of America*. New York, NY: G.P. Putnam's Sons, 2005.

USDA Dietary Guidelines 2005. January 12, 2005. Retrieved March 25, 2007 (http://www.health.gov/dietaryguidelines/dga2005/document/html/executivesummary.htm).

Index

About the Author

Stephanie Watson is a writer and editor based in Atlanta, Georgia. She has written or contributed to more than a dozen health and science books, including *Endometriosis, Encyclopedia of the Human Body: The Endocrine System, The Mechanisms of Genetics: An Anthology of Current Thought*, and *Science and Its Times*. Her work has also been featured on several health and wellness Web sites, including the Rosen Teen Health and Wellness database, for which she contributed several entries about eating disorders.

Photo Credits

Cover, p. 36 © www.istockphoto.com; p. 5 © AP Images; p. 8 © PR Newswire/Newscom; pp. 9, 22, 24 © Tim Boyle/Getty Images; p. 11 © Steve Vidler/SuperStock; p. 15 © Art Shay/Time & Life Pictures/Getty Images; p. 16 © Arnold Gold/New Haven Register/The Image Works; p. 18 © Peter Hvizdak/The Image Works; p. 20 © William Thomas/ Getty Images; p. 27 © www.istockphoto.com/steve vanhorn; p. 31 © age fotostock/SuperStock; p. 32 © Stephen Chernin/Getty Images; p. 38 © David Young-Wolff/PhotoEdit.

Designer: Tahara Anderson; **Editor:** Kathy Kuhtz Campbell
Photo Researcher: Amy Feinberg